The Great
Undoing

The Great
Undoing

Stuart Schwartz

NON-DUALITY PRESS
United Kingdom

NON-DUALITY PRESS
6 Folkestone Road Salisbury SP2 8JP United Kingdom
www.non-dualitybooks.com

For more information please visit the author's website:
www.satsangwithstuart.com

Cover design and interior layout:
Stuart Schwartz, Julian Noyce and John Gustard
Cover and interior photography: Alok Lawrence
Author photo: Sherry Burkart

Isbn 10: 0-9553999-8-X
Isbn 13: 978-0-9553999-8-5

Contents

Foreword

Most of Stuart's verse offerings included in this little book have arisen out of silence during the past few months, while others have appeared over a longer period of time. While the words and phrases themselves could not be more modern and colloquial, the poems have arranged themselves nicely into classical yogic themes: Vedanta's 'world-as-object' or *Illusion*; *Attachment* to the Illusion brought about by wrong identification with 'body/mind'; the separate, isolated *Me* as the centerpiece of limited, egoic 'becoming'; *Mind*, which is merely another word for thought which conditions all existence; and, finally *Awakening* to and in no-thing.

Some of the aphorisms are presented from the first person perspective of the individual who at times exults in new found freedom and at others awakens only to a new found appreciation of his or her awful predicament as a body/mind. Others bespeak teachings directly from the mouth of the Impersonal Itself. Whatever the form, these Western sutras are uncompromising in their spirit and message.

Like the terse poesy of the Indian sage Kabir whose verses startled me into immediate contemplation many years ago, the words on the pages that follow surprise the unsuspecting mind into silence. Characteristically, when asked, Stuart describes them simply as 'disarming.' To me they are both a map of Advaita's 'pathless path' and a statement beyond fact... Enough said!

Veda
Brookline, Massachusetts, July 2007

Introduction

Everything matters when I see myself as matter

Have you ever asked yourself, "Why can't I get to some state of balance, be content and stay there"? Here is what happened, you got lost. You diverted your attention from the wonder of 'being' to the meaning of the story—the story of your life—and then got lost in it. Instead of watching and enjoying the movie, you became a character with a life to live, with things to make happen, problems to solve, and responsibilities to inhabit it.

As a person, you can only be happy some of the time, and happiness seems to come only when circumstances are just right—just the way you want them to be. This is because as a separate entity joy is not inherent. It has to happen through something or someone else.

As persons we have to deal with emotional states of depression, disappointment, futility, pain, fear, desire, craving, outrage, disgust, self hatred, rejection, haughtiness, and happiness that we desperately try to hold on to.

Then there is the issue of our self image. How do we really feel about ourselves? Do we see ourselves as good or bad, valuable or worthless, powerful or weak, lucky or a loser, happy or despondent, bright or dim, desired or left out? And how do we try to disguise our own self-assessment and present ourselves outwardly?

Here is where we see each character locked into its perceived reality: feeling limited, begging for love; or screaming for the other to do what pleases them to prove that the other cares by not upsetting them; or nurturing to the extreme to manipulate the other; or pushing passionate living to the extreme to win some abstract contest because winning is the only option.

All of it becomes our habitual way of being that results in behavior that we regret, and ultimately becomes our warden. All one's beliefs, strategies for sustaining a life, all concepts, all conditioning, all sense of possibility; in fact, everything known and held to be true are congealed to the main belief "I am this person in this body: that is my identification." Now life reflects all that one is holding consciously and that which has been denied and stuffed away. We see ourselves everywhere we look. Now we are back in duality. It is all about me and my efforts to fix, change, improve, look for the end of suffering, and, in short, search for my happy, perfect life.

Many people, especially those on a spiritual path, believe that in order to be free one has to overcome these behaviors and become pure, and, at the same time, most believe that this is impossible. This isn't true. It just isn't so. Let the person be because submerged underneath all of it is your perfect Self.

We are all already awake, it is the natural state, and its nature is known when one is conscious of 'being' before clicking into identifying as the personal identity. This awakeness is the all pervading fullness of only 'Good' with no space left for anything else. From here all 'personal knowing' dissolves when seen, felt and fully faced. In this vast silence it is known that the body is a phantom taken for solid reality. Knowing this is seeing through the mystery of existence.

You are the strength, knowledge and impervious peace of being. Happiness stands alone in its natural state, and there is no way that it can end.

> 'If you let go of the I am the body idea,
> all of your problems will fly away'
> *Ramana Maharshi*

It is my desire that the words in this book bring you home.
—*Stuart*

Everything must be exactly
the way it is, as it occurs

One moment it is this way
another moment it is that way

all is karmic
and karma has nothing to do with you

All is a play that must be played out
and believed to be very very real

with consequences
severe and sublime

Striving keeps the dream going

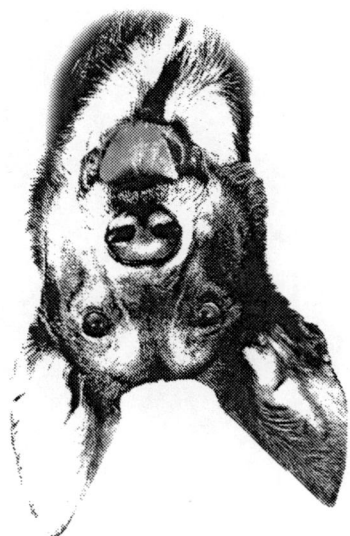

the illusion

appearances are always just appearances

Illusion is a play of characters
pretending not to be Self

You may appear to be feeble,
sick, young, healthy, wealthy, impoverished,
kind, arrogant, soulful or a sinner

No matter what you think or feel or believe,
none of this is who you are

You are playing a role, inhabiting a lifestyle,
losing yourself in your own life

What sounds true,
what feels true,
what you believe to be true,
is stopping you
from being the truth

When you are sleeping
absorbed in a dream
no one can convince you
that it is not real

I am as happy right now as I was
last Tuesday night when we were married
under the stars in Paris

And then I woke up

Tell me if you know the story I am
remembering fragments about
A soldier, or what was once a soldier,
no face left, or limbs for that matter

And

no way for him to express that all
was well, very, very well

You know how we are told
'don't judge by appearances'
Well that's what we do
when we believe

what we appear to be
is who we are

The only problems we have
are the problems we believe in

We are so attached to circumstance
that we think peace is
a result of resolution

Getting bored watching the lion
just sitting in a corner of the cage
My boy Jeremy said:
'Let's change the picture'

You are a character in a movie
You finally got the lead
Everyone you see is the supporting cast
Everything seen is on the screen of life
Your bedroom is backstage
Your closet is wardrobe
You have no choice but to awaken each day
and take on your role, even sick-days
Your words are scripted, you must speak them
You either witness and allow
or forget it's a movie and react
Then everything matters, big time

Better is better, isn't it?

Now you are a star with attitude
'What I say goes'

Who can argue with one who is asleep
to what they really are

Yes, you are the One and Only,
but just the same as everyone and everything
you see

...A spontaneous player
Enjoy!

You might want to see a better movie
but this is what's playing

All appears, feels real,
lasts awhile and disappears

Why is that so hard to see?

We see the other
as we see ourselves

Without the world
how would you know yourself?

Our world mimics reality
We honor higher awareness
We say 'Knowledge will set you free'
We celebrate union
Two becoming one heart

If only we could make it last forever...

Who would ever believe it is
all a smokescreen?

The senses camouflage reality
while
presence sees presence everywhere

We are here in this phenomenon,
we call it the world, reality,

because we believe that sustenance,
happiness and peace
lie somewhere
outside of ourselves

Catastrophe can crack
through the construct of the concept
that I am an individual
separate from the all

Sitting still watching the thoughts
appear and disappear can dissolve the delusion

There is only the moment,
this moment, this moment, this moment,
this moment, this moment,
this moment, this moment, this moment,
this moment, this moment,
this moment, this moment, this moment,
this moment, this moment,
this moment, this moment, this moment,
this moment, this moment,

this moment,

and no one owns it

No matter what is going on,
the background is total peace

Knowing

*all there is is Self,
and you are that*

is liberation

Whatever appears,
whatever you do,
wherever you go,

Stay home

theattachment

if the world wasn't so very, very real,
who would buy it, body and soul

Attachment
is the assumption
that what I see is real
and
it is the solidification
of the belief that
I am real

A whole life
can be spent identifying
as a man or a woman,

forgetting
to enjoy the intimacy
with one's essence
which ignites the form

Attachment
is buying the game of life
It is the process of fitting in,
knowing one's place,
learning the rules
and
breaking them

Attachment is the journey of
'getting ahead'

Even striving for enlightenment
is attachment

Attachment
is seeing the world
as the playground

Where is the
fun now?

Attachment is the exhilaration
of losing oneself in action,
loving the exhaustion that follows,
and wanting more

Attachment
is the process of latching onto
what we hope will
give us happiness and love,
not to mention security

And instead
always discovering
the unending limitation
of the temporal

The story of life is
desiring the other
to love us completely,

even if we can't

Believing that someone
or some system is 'the way'
is attachment

Honoring the forces
of good and evil
is attachment

Prejudice held
close to the heart
is attachment

Trying to clone yourself
into your children
is attachment

Whatever comes first
in your life
is your God

I love to be all love,
but give me what I want
when I want it

theme

individuality is a life sentence

I want to be free
but I want to be me,
free

How would I know myself
without the me?

Watch me
want a life with all the trimmings

Watch me want acknowledgment,
rewards and praise

Watch me afraid of blame,
hostility and shame

Watch me justify myself
Watch me be stoic and endure

Watch me demand my rights
Watch me suffer

Watch me try to modify my behavior
Watch me change

Watch me react
Watch me not react

Watch me allowing
Watch me fading out

Watch...

When I was a child
the battle cry was

'you must conform,'

what a gift in retrospect

My life was a rage exploding
There was no way anything could
reach my heart
I entered all the possibilities
and said no to everything

I used to say that so-and-so
took shallowness to new depths

I was so clever in my sandbox

One day it dawned on me
that the suffering wouldn't go away
no matter how right I was

I was waiting for God
to surrender to me

I have a son who tolerates me
and my ways

Yet he is afraid of being adrift

And
I have been a fool forever,
believing that
there were two of us

One morning in a Dublin
coffee shop my attention was
drawn to a sweet presence,
a radiance of well being

I had the sense that she knew
all of her needs
would always be met

She had strawberry hued hair
and porcelain skin
She was not yet two

The travesty is
that most love and hate
what appears to be
and ignore that which envelops us
in well-being

Have you ever noticed that many people
you reject have the same traits
you dislike in yourself,

while the goodness that you see
reflects your unfettered Self?

All resistance, opposition,
points of view, pain, power, praise,
blame, love, regret and success:

Everything matters
when I see myself as matter

Who is it
that believes that life
is an adventure?

Who is it that believes
all is possible?

Who is it that believes
justice will prevail?

Who is it that believes
all is for good purpose?

A person with good reason
not to be

just joy!

Every thought believed
solidifies the experience of 'me'

It is the belief that I am human
that keeps me glued to my life

Building a perfect life
piece by piece
is nothing more than
manipulating an image

You can count
on manipulation working
0% of the time
because
grace turns to gruel
in the manipulator's heart

It is the 'me' that is endlessly trying
to be the one and only

One must die to self-image,
and the very idea of separateness
or change the costume,

again

When we forget who we are
we react and fight for our lives

When we remember,
we see that there is no one
to fight and no issue of death

Happiness naturally reveals itself
when there is no me

the mind

*the mind knows everything except
what it is and where it is going*

Life is this business
of entertaining emotions
to protect oneself
from not existing

If you want to have a quiet mind,
don't listen

Imagine your life
being none of your business

The job at hand is
to eradicate the belief
that the mind can solve problems

It is the mind that is the
cause of all problems

The mind lulls one into discontent
Have no opinion for or against

Try it

All desires
try
to divert attention
from living in a state of
dispossession

Even the greatest
desire for freedom is squashed
when we refuse to face the depth of
our pain

Your mind is not your friend

Leave it alone

Don't take anything personally

Not even yourself

Do not bow down to false idols

What else is there?

Break loose from the bonds of reason
It's always a lose-lose proposition

Even if you get what you want,
what's next?

No trophy can make you happy
when you are not

One either rejoices just the way things are,
or one refuses to rejoice because
of the way things are

Each brings more of the same

Thought speaking:

I am the best,
the best of the best,
I deserve only adoration
and praise

...and then I'll let you
give me some more

Thought speaking:

You are the worst,
the worst of the worst,
there is no hope

I hear you,
I get it
Thank you,
I get it

You can't ever get the approval of the mind

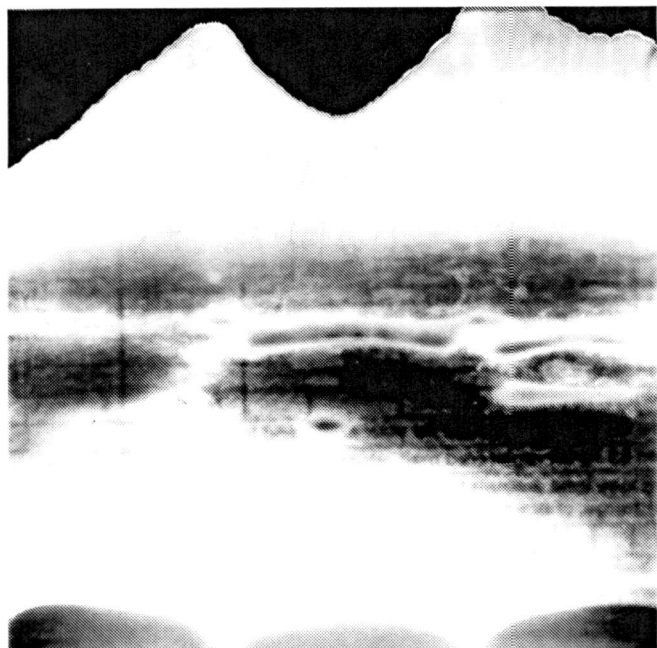

What you fear in the future
is what you are living now

The mind condemns
what is beyond its control
and understanding

When I believe my thoughts,
I am in chaos,
wanting peace

And
when I am silent,
I am the essence of everything

Only peace

Because our thoughts can create results
we believe that we are their cause

You have to leave your mind
to know the truth

If only I could take my desires
to the absolute!

.

You may be
100% right

And dead wrong

Do I want to be right?
Or
do I want to be free?

Oh my God,
what a decision!

theawakening

the world becomes real when you disappear

We are here
to discover
that who we think
is here
is not here
at all

I am not the one who has faltered
I AM

Absolute
appearance

beingness

seeing

beingness

being

Absolute
appearance

being

seeing

being

be

The most threatening thing
to human beings
is to not know themselves
as they know themselves

Improvement
is superfluous

Who you are is not what you
are trying to lift yourself
out of

Stop living in a state of mind
Step into a state of being

Leave yourself alone
Take a radical step and
Be no thing

To the one
who is well balanced, energetic,
honest, open, a top-of-the-game winner
and
to the unbalanced one,
immobilized by indecision,
also honest, open, and true,
but at the bottom of the game, a loser
and
everyone in between,
abiding by the rules of limitation

There are no favorites
when one is *being dreamed*

The great do-it-yourself project
is self-improvement

What if you really knew
there was no better life?

Your 'flaws' can be a gift
when you ride them in 'neutral'

Resistance to what is
causes us to see imperfection
everywhere,
within as well as without

When all flaws are accepted
the illusion of imperfection
dissolves in presence

One's greatest nemesis
seen through
is the entrance to heaven

The pursuit of happiness
is the cause of suffering

Those who think their actions
can make a difference
believe that bodies and minds are real

There is no solution
to the waking dream

To awaken
stay asleep
to the me

.

One can be consumed
by an emotional state,
one's very life,

and stop

Letting stillness absorb
every last trace

You can't fix duality,
but you *can* leave it alone

The moment is clean
until we obscure it
with our own point of view

Life takes care of everything that appears

...including you

Being quiet
is surrender

Surrender
is the backbone of joy

Allowing all to be as it is
even if it opposes your way
is love

Wisdom is not knowing
who you are
Only then can you be
vibrantly unprotected,
open and accepting
of all that occurs

What we could learn
from a tree

Leave behind
all you own,
all you believe,
all your desires

Just for now...

Enter an empty second,
get lost in the infinite,
meander to *godknowswhere*

In silence you will discover
that whatever is necessary
to say, or do, or have
appears

Choose that which ends all sorrows
Leave behind the one that knows
Then,
choose to ignore the one
who chooses

The great undoing is
dissolving the 'me'
into the infinite

Listen and be Silent

(Note how "Listen" and "Silent" share the same letters)

As a person
thoughts are believed to be true

As Self thoughts are seen
to have nothing to do with you

The mother stares through
the son's shame

and

the beauty of being
is revealed

Prior to all understanding,
contentment is natural

Knowing this,
there is nothing to prove

Everyone is your mirror
There are those with whom you agree
and those with whom you don't
Some you love and others
you think should perish
At times your heart can burst with joy
or cower from heartbreak

All are parts of our make up,
vying for supremacy
We are busy entertaining or denying,
speaking forth, or numb and cold
Our positions are our code of being

Put the mirror down

Be Silent...Whole

Resurrection happens by itself

This grace is you

Honor everything
Let everything be exactly the way it is
Honor all, and leave all alone

Let pain persist
Allow rage to roar,
tension to taunt,
and anxiety to annihilate
If you can do this,
all the illusory guards
blocking God will die

What will be left, my friend,
is the fearless state

The end of the fear of love

Acknowledgements

Thanks to all the writers, poets, friends, and family who shared of themselves so freely.

Claire Daniel, Meriel Hoare, Janet Kaplan, Steve Katz, Alok Lawrence, Mukti Marcom, Kim Rylander, Jason Schwartz, Walter Stone, Morag Donnelly

and a very special thank you to Veda who contributed so much Presence, brilliance and editing skill

Humble gratitude to the Ones who inspired and acknowledged

Lester Levenson
'How long should it take an Infinite Being to realize their nature?'

Robert Adams
'There is only the liberated Self, and you are that'.

to all my sons

and thank you to all the people in my life who insisted that I inhabit the role I was supposed to portray, as they saw it. They know who they are.

Printed in the United States
96903LV00001B/37-39/A